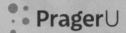

PragerU is redefining how people think about media and education. Watched millions of times every day, PragerU is the world's leading nonprofit with educational, entertaining, pro-American videos for every age. From intellectual, fact-based 5-Minute Videos and powerful personal storytelling to animated shows made just for kids—PragerU helps people of all ages think and live better.

PragerU Kids teaches history, civics, financial literacy, and American values to children across the K-12th grade spectrum. With kids shows, books, and educational resources for every grade, PragerU Kids offers content that parents and teachers trust and children love. Watch for free and learn more at PragerUkids.com.

Published by PragerU

15021 Ventura Boulevard #552

Sherman Oaks, CA 91403

Arrival

Near Olean, New York, Winter 1797

With careful steps, John Chapman climbed the snowbank. The icy wind nipped his ears, his brow, the tip of his nose. When he saw the far-off cabin—a brown square with snow on the roof and a stone chimney—he broke into a grin.

Finally, he thought, pulling the thin cloak tighter. John turned and called back to his half-brother, Nathaniel, who was only twelve.

When the two left their house in Massachusetts a year ago, they had no idea the family hideaway in the mountains would be this hard to reach. They'd walked a long way on foot, but the brushes with hunger and freezing cold had not slowed them down—just the opposite. Here, with the bleached mountains, the wind, and the promise of cheap land due west, John's heart was soaring.

Nathaniel coughed next to him. "Is that it? Did we reach the cabin?"

John nodded. Hearing Nathaniel shiver brought a hollow feeling to his stomach. *Could they both make it?* Having pushed this far into the **frontier**, could he and Nathaniel survive in such a harsh place? Some rest and a warm, crackling fire would help. After that, and if they could hang on until spring, they would keep moving.

"Come on," John said, staggering forward.

Hundreds of winters later, Americans know John Chapman by a different name—Johnny Appleseed. Today, he's a legend of history and a symbol of America's pioneering spirit.

Meet Johnny Appleseed

Much of Johnny Appleseed's story is a **tall tale**, but not all of it. Bare facts paint the picture of a man who lived outdoors, helped others by planting apple trees, and bravely explored the frontier. With his **entrepreneurial spirit**, this man inspired the legend through everyday action.

Long before he became "Appleseed John" (as some first called him), John Chapman was part of a large family. He was born on September 26 in 1774, almost two years before the signing of the Declaration of Independence. His father, Nathaniel, fought in the Revolution, and his mother, Elizabeth, died when he was young. After his father remarried, the family grew with ten more children—including his half-brother Nathaniel. By the time John and Nathaniel left for the frontier, everyone had been living in a house no bigger than a small modern apartment!

Thinking of cheap land and probably eager for more elbow room, the half-brothers joined a wave of people heading for the **Northwest Territory**. In the thick of a freezing cold winter, John and Nathaniel struggled over the rough **Allegheny** Mountains to the family's tiny cabin. Reports of newcomers securing free land in Ohio's hills and valleys sounded too good to be true. To young men like them, the unsettled frontier meant freedom. Opportunity. A chance to build the future you wanted... as long as you could survive the winter.

Frontier Facts:

 In the early 1800s, the unpopulated frontier included modern-day Ohio, Indiana, Illinois, Michigan, Wisconsin, and Minnesota. By 1840, about seven million people (or forty percent of America's population) were living in this region.

 Right before John was born, the **Ohio Company** started offering settlers a hundred free acres in the "Donation Tract" (Central Ohio). To claim their land, settlers had three years to plant fifty apple trees and twenty peach trees.

 Life on the frontier was hard and dangerous. In that time period, boys were often married by age seventeen and girls by age fourteen. Men had a **life expectancy** of thirty-four years old.

 One out of every four children on the frontier died before the age of twenty-one. Diseases like smallpox, malaria, and scarlet fever were common. Areas as big as three million acres often had only one trained doctor.

 To treat pain or illness, people like John Chapman turned to plants.

- Catnip for stomach ache.
- Fennel for indigestion.
- Horehound for coughs or a cold.
- Mullein for a sore throat.
- Pennyroyal to help women giving birth.
- Rattlesnake root for—you guessed it—snakebites.
- Water from creeks and rivers made people sick. To stay hydrated, people drank whiskey or alcoholic cider made from apples.

AMERICA
IN THE TIME OF
JOHNNY
APPLESEED

Frontier Businessman

The brothers survived... *barely*. Nathaniel almost starved, and it's possible that passing Indians saved his life. A few years later, John Chapman walked into a **general store** in western Pennsylvania. The store's record tells us that two young men made several purchases that year. They might have been living along the nearby creek where some think John planted his first apple tree **nursery**.

When the rest of the family came out to Ohio, Nathaniel joined them—but John kept going. For the rest of his life, he explored the rugged frontier without settling down. When the frontier moved through Pennsylvania, Ohio, and Indiana, John moved with it. Wherever he went, he planted, bought land, and **bartered** seeds and trees for goods he needed. Influenced by the teachings of **Emanuel Swedenborg**, he shared his Christian faith with everyone he met.

The "Appleseed" nickname stuck because John always carried seeds with him. In a region where raising apple and peach trees secured the ownership of land, seeds were **start-up capital**. By planting and selling apple trees in areas where settlers were arriving, John filled an important need.

Over time, helping newcomers survive and hang on to their land became his calling card. The rumors of his kindness, outdoor skills, and unusual appearance grew as tall as the trees he planted.

Why Apples?

Here's why apple orchards were so important on the frontier:

Settlers could use them to claim land. Planting and growing orchards for five years was a common part of a land contract. It showed that someone was serious about **cultivating** a piece of land.

Apples were a key ingredient. On the frontier, people used them to make vinegar, cider for drinking, and products like apple butter. With little **hard currency**, people traded goods, products, and even apple trees for other supplies.

Apple cider was safe to drink. Cider, like most alcohol, has disinfectant properties that kill bacteria. People on the frontier knew that drinking cider was safer than drinking water from creeks or streams.

Apples grown directly from seeds were not usually eaten. The trees that John planted produced small, bitter apples that people mashed up for cider. Some called these apples "spitters" because of their taste.

Apple trees could be grafted to produce sweet fruit. To grow edible fruit, settlers **grafted** trees. That means they joined an upper, mature part of a fruit-bearing tree (called a *scion*) to the lower part of another tree (called the *rootstock*). When the two parts grew together, the tree would produce the same variety of fruit as the upper part.

Orchards reminded settlers of home. The frontier was wild and dangerous, but apple orchards reminded people of New England.

Apples were "nature's toothbrush." Before toothbrushes were common, it was believed that eating something crunchy and fibrous like an apple could help clean your teeth.

A Familiar Name

Jacob's Creek, Southwestern Pennsylvania, Fall 1806

Slop, slop, slop.

William rubbed his eyes and looked again. In the middle of the heaps of mashed apple pulp, a lean, scrawny man was sitting cross-legged. Both of his hands were wrist-deep in a pile of pulp, and when he moved them around, the *slop, slop* resumed.

As William crept closer, he saw that the young man had bare, **calloused** feet and rags for clothes. He could be no more than twenty-five. With long, wild hair, a mossy beard, and caked dirt all over his back, he looked homeless. Had he been living outdoors? William noticed the half-full burlap sack. Every so often, people stopped to pick through the mill's trash for unused apple seeds.

When the young man stood, his clothes hung loose. He slung the sack over his shoulder and picked up a young **sapling** with its roots tied in a sack.

"I'm John," he said, handing the sapling over. "For your trouble."

They shook hands. William did not recognize him, and yet the calm voice, gentle eyes, and rugged appearance seemed familiar. *Was this the man they called Appleseed John?*

"I've heard about you," William said. "You're the one who sleeps outdoors and protects animals. Indians think you're a medicine man. That true?"

"Sure," the young man chuckled. "Want to hear a story?"

Larger Than Life

Wherever he went, "Johnny Appleseed" stole the show. People claimed he wore no shoes, a coffee sack for a shirt, and a tin cooking pot on his head. They said he loved animals so much that he gave up a perfectly good sleeping spot for bear cubs. In another **rumor**, John put out his evening campfire so the mosquitos would not fly into it.

John's love for animals was one **conviction** people found strange. As a Swedenborg follower, he believed God's presence rested in all living things. He would not fight, carry a weapon, or cut trees to grow better apples. These beliefs probably raised eyebrows, but people respected John for living them out.

With the land as his home, John's endurance was remarkable. He even won respect from the skilled Indian warriors living in the Great Lakes Region. Unlike settlers who dealt with the frontier's harshness by getting drunk or violent, John's gentleness was a shining example. Being tough and self-reliant allowed him to be generous. Sometimes, when a person could not pay for his seeds or trees, he gave them away for free.

For a man who could walk ten or twenty miles alone, John still loved company. He preached the Bible wherever he went, but he also told whopping stories about himself. To entertain children, he gave out ribbons and stuck pins in his calloused feet.

In a place full of wild characters, it's incredible that a peaceful **evangelist** became such a legend.

GREAT LAKES
ANIMALS

RATTLESNAKE
RATTLE

RATTLESNAKE
FANGS

GREAT LAKES RATTLER

A dark-colored rattlesnake native to the Great
Lakes region. The snake is now endangered,
possibly because hunters were once paid a
bounty for killing them. When people heard that
Johnny Appleseed felt no pain when a snake bit
his foot, they probably pictured this rattler.

BOBCAT TRACKS

WOLVERINE

WOLVERINE
TRACKS

A fierce, brown-furred weasel. Wolverines
are lonesome scavengers who feed on
berries, plants, and carrion (dead, rotting
animals). They can also hunt large prey
like deer and moose.

BOBCAT

A slender, spotted "wild cat." Nocturnal and
adaptable, bobcats hunt rabbits, chickens,
geese, and small rodents within their territory.

A FIELD GUIDE TO
GREAT LAKES
PLANTS

BLUE VIOLET

A colorful blue or lilac flower that grows throughout the Great Lakes region. Since 1908, the blue violet has been the state flower of Illinois.

SUGAR MAPLE

A thin, well-loved tree of the Great Lakes and the Northeast. Sugar maple leaves turn brilliant shades of yellow and orange in the fall. Canadians love them for the sticky, sugary product made from their sap: maple syrup.

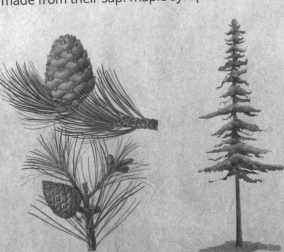

MICHIGAN WHITE PINE

Michigan's state tree is a majestic one. Tall and stately, the white pine is covered in green needles that deer and other animals love to munch, especially in winter.

"A volunteer was asked for and a tall, lank man said, 'I'll go.' He was bareheaded, barefooted, and unarmed. His manner was meek and you had to look the second time into his clear, blue eyes to fully fathom the courage and determination shown in their depths."

-Biographer A.J. Baughman

Fly For Your Lives!

Near Mount Vernon, Ohio, September 1812

When he heard whispering, John crept off the trail.

Who was this? British scouts? Bandits? A pair of Tecumseh's feared **Shawnee** warriors? In the thick darkness, John could not tell.

He heard footsteps. The voices on the trail were now talking.

He pressed his face against the rough hide of an oak tree, making himself so narrow nobody could spot him. His lungs were on fire, but John held his breath. The past three hours of running, wading through creeks, and knocking on cabin doors to warn people were a heavy blur. He kept thinking of the men he'd spoken to before accepting the task. Men gathered outside with torches, faces glowing with worry. *Mount Vernon*, they'd said. *Someone has to warn Captain Douglas the British forces are coming... and that the Indians are out for revenge.*

When the talking died down, John peeked around.

Moving was risky... but he *had* to keep going.

Marathon Man

One evening in September of 1812, John Chapman volunteered for a dangerous mission—walking nearly thirty miles at night to warn the town of Mount Vernon, and people who lived nearby, of a coming British attack.

John's mission came right in the nick of time. A few months earlier, the United States had declared war on England, and the conflict known as **The War of 1812** was raging around the country. To make matters worse, U.S. forces at Fort Detroit had surrendered to the British without fighting, and this left British forces wide open to cross Lake Erie and launch an attack on Ohio. **Wyandot** Indians who wanted revenge after a U.S. militia raided one of their villages were rumored to be joining them—and many in the surrounding areas had no idea. The people who sent John worried that Indians, the British, or *both*, were already coming for them.

Because he knew the terrain, John stepped up. That night, he reportedly ran more than twenty-six miles—the distance of a **marathon**—to Mount Vernon. One account has him knocking on doors and shouting: *"Fly! Fly! For your lives! They are murdering at Mansfield!"* At cabin after cabin, he stopped to warn people like **Paul Revere**, who rode his horse through Massachusetts thirty-seven years earlier during the **Revolutionary War** to warn colonists of the approaching British.

But unlike Paul Revere, John had no horse. On foot, and in pitch darkness, John carried the message all the way to Mount Vernon. Some think he made it there and *back* by sunrise.

Mansfield

Mountains

Scale of Miles

Mansfield

Mount Vernon

Mount Vernon

STATE OF
OHIO

A Pioneering Spirit

John's heroic run is well-remembered. But he's also known for preaching the Gospel as a frontier evangelist. John's faith grew to a raging fire during the **Great Awakening**—a Christian revival that swept America in the early 1800s. Wherever he went, John shared God's word and Swedenborg's teachings. Some claim that he gave out gospel tracts that he carried in his tin hat.

Near the end of John's life, things grew harder. A **recession** in 1819 forced him to sell much of the land he owned to survive. With few people able to pay him, he accepted IOU notes—promises to be paid back in the future. As John turned sixty, staying on the frontier's edge where settlers needed apple trees was challenging. Even though he eventually owned 15,000 trees in Indiana, he was never able to stay in one place. He never married or had a family.

John Chapman died of pneumonia at a friend's house in Fort Wayne, Indiana. It was March of 1845, just sixteen years before the Civil War. By that time, the tales of "Johnny Appleseed" had taken on a life of their own.

Over time, John came to embody America's **pioneering spirit**. While he never won a military medal or turned his business **enterprise** into a huge profit, his life is legendary. John's resilience, independent spirit, and generosity remind us of the brave souls who came out and opened up the frontier for everyone else. At a time when a fresh start meant facing the wild unknown, John paved the way by demonstrating **stewardship**. Today, his life helps people appreciate nature and support **conservation** efforts.

Thanks to him, having faith, relying on yourself, and helping others are not just ways to survive the winter.

They are as American as apple pie.

GREAT LAKES
WEAPONRY & TECHNOLOGY

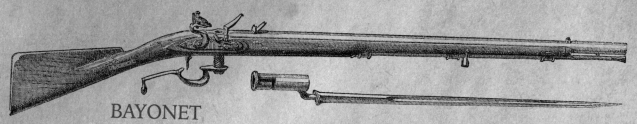

BAYONET

A blade that may be fixed to the muzzle of a firearm. A valuable weapon for soldiers during the War of 1812, especially when their muskets needed reloading.

GIMLET

John Chapman purchased a gimlet—a small, hand-held wooden drill—from a general store in 1797. Pioneers used gimlets to drill holes, build fences, and shape wood in useful ways.

SCREW PRESS

This old invention found new life on the Ohio frontier. A bucket filled with apples sits beneath a heavy weight or "press" attached to a screw. Tightening the screw crushes the apples into pulp and juice—step one in making alcoholic cider.

Make Your Own Homemade Applesauce!

Ingredients

- 4 large Pink Lady apples peeled, cored, and cut into small chunks
- 1/3 cup water
- 1/4 cup granulated sugar (may substitute with unrefined sugar such as honey, maple syrup, or coconut sugar)
- 1 tablespoon fresh lemon juice (about half a lemon)
- 1 teaspoon ground cinnamon
- 1/8 teaspoon salt

Instructions

- Place all of the ingredients in a medium saucepan and stir well.
- Bring to a boil over medium heat, and reduce heat slightly. Cover and cook 30 minutes, or until the apples are very soft.
- Mash with a potato masher or the back of a spoon until the applesauce is the desired consistency. Serve and enjoy!

Fact or Legend?

The Johnny Appleseed legend is filled with juicy exaggerations.
If you've read closely or if you've done your own research, you can figure out
which statements about him are FACT or LEGEND.

When you've got your answers written down, check the answers at the end of the book.

1. Johnny Appleseed walked many miles without shoes. _____

2. Johnny Appleseed wore a heavy iron skillet on his head as protection from
   Indian arrows. _____

3. Indians on the frontier respected him. Some considered him a "medicine man"
   with the power to summon magic. _____

4. Johnny Appleseed was born in 1774, just before the American
   Revolutionary War. _____

5. Johnny Appleseed could chop down as many trees as two men...
   and just as fast. _____

6. Johnny Appleseed once floated hundreds of miles down a river on a large hunk
   of ice. _____

7. Johnny Appleseed was very generous and sometimes gave away apple trees
   for free. _____

8. The bottoms of his feet were so tough that when a rattlesnake bit them, he felt
   no pain whatsoever. _____

9. Johnny Appleseed's orchards grew tart, bitter apples used for cider,
   not sweet ones. _____

10. Johnny Appleseed once hid from Indian warriors by lying down in a swamp and
    taking a nap—with his face out of the water so he could breathe. _____

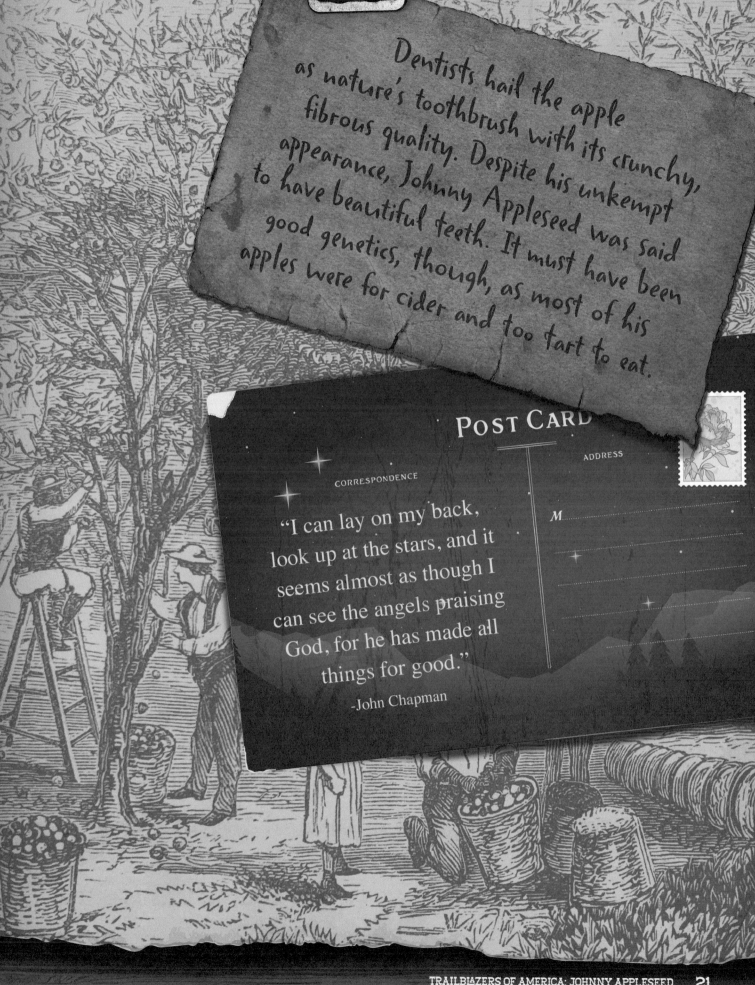

Dentists hail the apple as nature's toothbrush with its crunchy, fibrous quality. Despite his unkempt appearance, Johnny Appleseed was said to have beautiful teeth. It must have been good genetics, though, as most of his apples were for cider and too tart to eat.

POST CARD

CORRESPONDENCE

ADDRESS

M

"I can lay on my back, look up at the stars, and it seems almost as though I can see the angels praising God, for he has made all things for good."

-John Chapman

John Chapman's Travels*

After the Prohibition era from 1920-1933, the apple industry began to reinvent itself. It focused on the health benefits of eating apples. This is when the phrase, "An apple a day keeps the doctor away," became popular.

All the counties where John Chapman had apple orchards

5 1845. Died in Fort Wayne, Indiana.

OHIO

*Locations on the map are likely but not definite based on best records available.

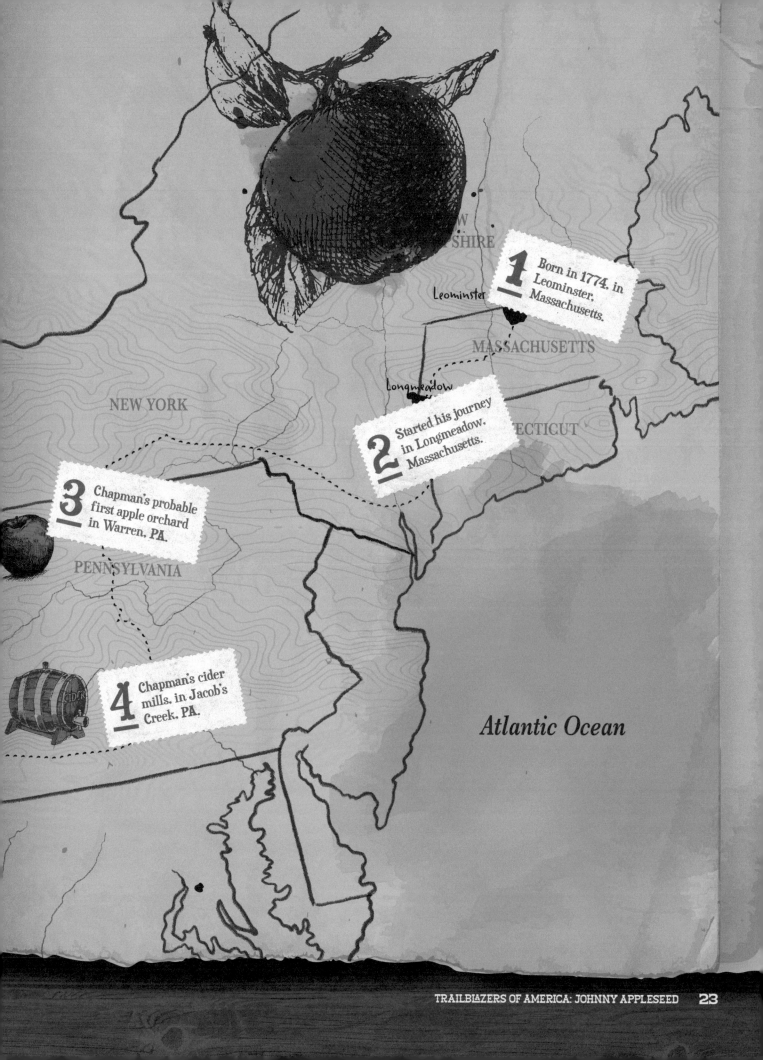

NEW HAMPSHIRE

Leominster

1 Born in 1774, in Leominster, Massachusetts.

MASSACHUSETTS

Longmeadow

NEW YORK

2 Started his journey in Longmeadow, Massachusetts.

CONNECTICUT

3 Chapman's probable first apple orchard in Warren, PA.

PENNSYLVANIA

4 Chapman's cider mills, in Jacob's Creek, PA.

Atlantic Ocean

Largest Daily
Circulation
In New York

WORD SEARCH

VOL. 127 - NO. 39

PRICE 10 CEN'

There are reported to be as many as 200 varieties of apples grown in America today. Over 90% are grown in the state of Washington. The top 10 varieties are Red Delicious, Gala, Granny Smith, Honeycrisp, Fuji, Golden Delicious, Braeburn, Pink Lady, Jonagold, and Rome. Find these apple names in the word search below.

```
U A R J Z I B D A T Y L T F D R G
G X G G N R U B E A R B K U S J O
N S W M E A B C U X T D L J G O L
C D D S F B T E R Z K P F I G M D
J F Z W F N H A J R N X M B V E E
M X U Q B Y V A L K I H W G Z F N
N C F S X W T D G A X W U T Y H D
Z R M U D Q Z A V P G H H Z T P E
G S U O I C I L E D D E R I J Y L
V M U G V K H Q K E W N M O R L I
D P S I R C Y E N O H S N O Z A C
G J P I N K L A D Y Y A M O Q L I
G L F T R A L Q T N G E H N I P O
P J R X Q Q J A N O F H J F C O U
F W M Y A J E A L U P K M E L I S
S A I U M Q R D U K R L Y G K D X
E D O F J G S Q H K Q I U Z T C A
```

See answers on page 29

"God talked to him through every tree, every leaf, every rock, every beast great and small, every atom of creation."

-Author Howard Means

Writing Task

What did you learn from Johnny Appleseed's story?

How did he embody the American spirit?

_____

_____

_____

_____

_____

_____

_____

_____

_____

_____

_____

_____

_____

_____

_____

_____

_____

_____

_____

_____

Glossary

Allegheny: A region of the Eastern United States, including the Allegheny River and Allegheny Mountains, which are part of the Appalachian Mountain Range. Some believe the name comes from a Native American word meaning "fine river" or "beautiful river."

Barter: To trade goods or products directly for other goods or products. Before currencies like the American dollar were widely used, people on the frontier bartered with whiskey, leather goods, or even apple trees.

Calloused: Hardened skin developed from repeated use or exposure, common among people who do physical labor like farming or building.

Conservation: Efforts taken to protect animal species from extinction, or protect and restore natural habitats.

Conviction: Strongly held belief or firm opinion. Convictions influence someone's actions and decisions.

Cultivate: To prepare and use land for raising crops.

Emanuel Swedenborg: A Swedish Christian theologian who emphasized spiritual visions and study of the natural world. Swedenborg's teachings were adopted by small churches and communities in Pennsylvania and throughout the United States during the early 1800s.

Entrepreneurial Spirit: The motivation and willingness to develop, organize, and manage a business venture despite risks and challenges. An entrepreneur is a person who starts and runs a business, taking on financial risks in the hope of profit.

Enterprise: A difficult project or undertaking.

Evangelist: A person who seeks to convert others to the Christian faith, often traveling from place to place to preach.

Frontier: The edge of settled land. In America during the 1800s, the term often referred to land west of the Mississippi River, where pioneers would move to start new lives and communities.

General Store: A retail store common in small towns, especially on the frontier, that sells a wide variety of goods needed by the community.

Grafting: Joining two plants together to grow as one. This technique helps improve plants like apple trees, allowing them to grow better fruit.

The Great Awakening: Two periods in American history when belief in Christianity greatly increased. John Chapman was influenced by the Second Great Awakening, around the late 1700s and early 1800s, which emphasized large gatherings and moral issues like slavery and women's rights.

Hard Currency: Money that was originally made from, or backed, by precious metals like gold and silver. Today, currencies like the American dollar are no longer backed by silver and gold, but they are called "hard currency" when a nation is politically and economically stable.

Life Expectancy: The average number of years a person is expected to live. This varied widely in the 1800s due to different living conditions and medical knowledge.

Marathon: Originally, a long-distance race of about 26 miles; can also refer to any task or activity that requires prolonged effort.

Northwest Territory: A region of the early United States encompassing present-day Ohio, Indiana, Illinois, Michigan, Wisconsin, and part of Minnesota. It was significant for its early governance under the Northwest Ordinance of 1787, which outlawed slavery in the territory. This also set a precedent for the establishment of public education and supported freedom of worship, laying foundational principles for future American expansion.

Nursery: Place where plants, especially young trees and shrubs, are grown for sale or for planting elsewhere.

Ohio Company: An 18th-century land speculation company that sold land along the frontier cheaply.

Paul Revere: An American silversmith and a patriot in the American Revolution. Paul Revere is famous for his midnight ride to alert the colonial militia of approaching British forces.

Pioneering Spirit: The attitude and determination of people willing to endure hardships to explore new territories and create new opportunities.

Recession: A period of economic decline when businesses and consumers spend less money, often leading to higher unemployment.

Revolutionary War: A war fought between the thirteen American colonies and Great Britain from 1775 to 1783. During the war, the colonies fought to gain independence from British rule and joined together to sign the Declaration of Independence in 1776.

Rumor: A piece of information or a story that is passed from person to person but has not been confirmed as true.

Sapling: A young tree, especially one that is small and just starting to grow, often used in reference to new growth and potential.

Shawnee: A Native American tribe originally from the Ohio Valley region, known for their resistance against European-American settlers on their land.

Startup Capital: Money or resources used to start a new enterprise.

Stewardship: The responsible management of something entrusted to one's care, such as the environment or property.

Tall Tale: A greatly exaggerated, sometimes humorous story that tells the feats of a larger-than-life hero. Tall tales are common in American folklore.

War of 1812: A war fought by Great Britain and the United States from 1812 to 1815. Even though Great Britain burned the White House and joined Native American allies against the United States, the Battle of New Orleans was a resounding U.S. victory.

Wyandot: A Native American tribe that resided in the northeastern woodlands of the United States. Wyandots spoke the Iroquoian language.

Sources

D, Louisa. "Johnny Appleseed's Legacy Lives on in Fort Wayne." *Visit Fort Wayne.com*. 02 August 2023. https://www.visitfortwayne .com/blog/stories/post/johnny-appleseed-legacy-lives- on-in-fort-wayne. Accessed November 2023.

Gannon, Kim & Kent Walter. "The Lord is Good to Me (Johnny Appleseed)." *Disney Clips*. 1948. https://www.disneyclips.com/lyrics/ lyricsmelodytime3.html. Accessed November 2023.

Geiling, Natasha. "The Real Johnny Appleseed Brought Apples—and Booze to the American Frontier." *The Smithsonian*. 10 November 2014. https://www.smithsonianmag.com/arts-culture/real-johnny- appleseed-brought-applesand-booze-american-frontier-180953263/. Accessed November 2023.

Hoagland, Edward. "Johnny Appleseed." *American Heritage*. December 1979. https://www.americanheritage.com/johnny-appleseed. Accessed November 2023.

Kelly, Kate. "Johnny Appleseed Debunked." *America Comes Alive*. https://americacomesalive.com/johnny-appleseed-debunked/. Accessed November 2023.

Marcie. "Easy Homemade Applesauce Recipe." *Flavor the Moments*. 5 October 2021. https://flavorthemoments.com/pink-lady-applesauce/. Accessed November 2023.

Means, Howard. *Johnny Appleseed: The Man, the Myth, the American Story*. Simon and Schuster, 2012.

Synan, Mariel. "Who Was Johnny Appleseed." *History.com*. 10 May 2023. https://www.history.com/news/who-was-johnny-appleseed. Accessed November 2023.

The Editors of Encyclopedia Britannica. "Johnny Appleseed: American Nurseryman." *Britannica.com*. 31 October 2023. https://www.britannica.com/biography/John-Chapman. Accessed November 2023.

The Editors of Encyclopedia Britannica. "The Second Great Awakening." *Britannica.com*. 15 November 2023. https://www.britannica.com/ topic/Second-Great-Awakening. Accessed November 2023.

Tristan, David. "September 26, 1774—Johnny Appleseed: a real man, a real person." *ABC27.com*. 26 September 2023. https://www.abc27.com /history/sept-26-1774-johnny-appleseed-a-real-person-a-real- tall-tale/. Accessed November 2023.

WA Apple. "The Story of Johnny Appleseed." *Waapple.org*. https://waapple.org/johnny-appleseed/. Accessed November 2023.

Image Credit: Laurin Rinder / Shutterstock.com

Fact or Legend?

1. FACT
2. LEGEND
3. FACT
4. FACT
5. LEGEND
6. LEGEND
7. FACT
8. LEGEND
9. FACT
10. LEGEND

Word Search

```
U A R J Z I B D A T Y L T F D R G
G X G G N R U B E A R B K U S J O
N S W M A B C U X T D L J G O L
C D D S F B T E R Z K P F I G M D
J F Z W F N H A J R N X M B V E
M X U Q B Y V A L K I H W G Z F N
N C F S X W T D G A X W U T Y H D
Z R M U D Q Z A V P G H H Z T P E
G S U O I C I L E D D E R I J Y L
V M U G V K H Q K E W N M O R L I
D P S I R C Y E N O H S N O Z A C
G J P I N K L A D Y Y A M O Q L I
G L F T R A L Q T N G E H N I P O
P J R X Q Q J A N O F H J F C O U
F W M Y A J E A L U P K M E L I S
S A I U M O R D U K R L Y G K D X
E D O F J G S Q H K Q I U Z T C A
```

READY FOR MORE?

Experience all the **FREE CONTENT** PragerU Kids has to offer!

STREAM FREE SHOWS ON YOUR TV OR TABLET

Download our FREE mobile or TV app to stream every PragerU Kids show! Or, watch any time at PragerUkids.com.

ENJOY HOURS OF FREE SHOWS

Browse over 300 educational videos for K-12, including game shows, cartoons, and inspiring reality shows.

EXPLORE WHOLESOME STORIES & AMAZING HISTORY

Download free e-books at PragerUkids.com or purchase printed copies on Amazon.

FREE RESOURCES FOR TEACHERS & PARENTS

Supplement your child's viewing experience with lesson plans & worksheets that meet educational standards.

Experience Fun, Interactive, and Educational Content at
PRAGERUKIDS.COM

Made in United States
Troutdale, OR
05/16/2025